EMIs Made Easy
for
MRCPsych Exam

Dedicated to my parents

EMIs Made Easy
for
MRCPsych Exam

Dr Madhu Selvaraj

Printed in Victoria, Canada

Note for Librarians: a cataloguing record for this book that includes Dewey Classification and US Library of Congress numbers is available from the National Library of Canada. The complete cataloguing record can be obtained from the National Library's online database at:
www.nlc-bnc.ca/amicus/index-e.html
ISBN 1-4120-2686-5

TRAFFORD

This book was published on-demand in cooperation with Trafford Publishing.
On-demand publishing is a unique process and service of making a book available for retail sale to the public taking advantage of on-demand manufacturing and Internet marketing. On-demand publishing includes promotions, retail sales, manufacturing, order fulfilment, accounting and collecting royalties on behalf of the author.

Suite 6E, 2333 Government St., Victoria, B.C. V8T 4P4, CANADA
Phone 250-383-6864   Toll-free 1-888-232-4444 (Canada & US)
Fax 250-383-6804   E-mail sales@trafford.com   Web site www.trafford.com
TRAFFORD PUBLISHING IS A DIVISION OF TRAFFORD HOLDINGS LTD
Trafford Catalogue #04-0514   www.trafford.com/robots/04-0514.html

13   12   11   10   9   8   7   6   5   4   3   2

Contents

Acknowledgements

I would like to express my profound gratitude to the following for their helpful comments and advice:

Dr A Gandhi, Dr D Gunatilake, Dr T Joshi, Dr M Kulatunga, Dr A Malik, Dr R Paranthaman, Dr P Peddu, Dr M Vemuri, Dr M Yousuf,

And
To my Tutors

Dr P Allman, Dr W Conlon , Dr R Eggar, Dr K Gingell, Dr M Kurian, Dr H Lloyd , Dr M Slowik, & Dr V Staples.

I would like to thank my colleagues of Stonebow Unit Hereford, Bushey Fields Hospital Dudley, ELMS Halesowen and SuperEgo café forum members for their support and help.

I also would like to thank Trafford Publishing services for their invaluable technical support and advice.

Preface

There have been several changes to the MRCPsych exam format over the past couple of years and one of the most important is the introduction of extended matching items (EMIs). Another hurdle to this already difficult to pass exam!

This book contains 80 EMI themes selected from various specialities of psychiatry distributed as 8 exam papers each containing 10 themes. Though important topics might contain more themes, they don't represent the distribution of the themes in the actual membership exam.

A subject wise index is given at the end of the questions. Though I believe that the candidates of both parts of the exam may find all the themes useful, the readers of part 1 and part 2 may want to choose the themes relevant for their exam from the index.

It's hoped that the readers will find this material useful in other parts of the MRCPsych examinations. I wish you good luck for the exam.

Madhu Selvaraj
April 2004.

Caution to the readers

While every effort has been taken in the preparation of this book to ensure reasonable coverage of the subject matter and the accuracy of answers & references, the author accepts no responsibility for loss arising out of such errors that might subsequently be found in this book.

LIST OF THEMES

Paper 1

1) Alcohol Related Problems

2) Neuropharmacology - Side Effects

3) Concepts in Psychotherapy

4) Treatment of Motor Disorders

5) Theories in Psychology

6) Neurological Signs

7) Diagnosis of Stupor

8) Phenomenology

9) Pharmacokinetics

10) Mechanism of Action of Receptors

Paper 2

11) Schools of Psychoanalytic Theory

12) Motor Disorders in Schizophrenia

13) Concepts in Attachment

14) Learning Disability

15) Diagnosis of Cognitive Impairment

16) Side Effects of Lithium

17) Somatoform Disorders

18) Management of Side Effects

19) Basic Psychopharmacology

20) Hyperactivity in Children

1)   THEME: ALCOHOL RELATED PROBLEMS

Options

    A. Outpatient detoxification programme
    B. Inpatient detoxification programme
    C. Disulfiram
    D. Acamprosate
    E. Multivitamins
    F. Motivational interviewing
    G. Dynamic psychotherapy
    H. Relapse prevention measures
    I. No medical treatment required

Select TWO options from the above list for each of the following questions that are more appropriate in the management of this patient. Each option may be used once, more than once or not at all.

1. A 55-year-old healthy married man has been drinking heavily for the past 2 years. Following deterioration in his marital relationship, he is now willing to stop drinking and asks for help. His wife is pleased with his decision and willing to support him.

2. After a period of abstinence, he started drinking again and his wife has left him. His neighbour was concerned by his deterioration in self-care and took him to his GP. He appears very malnourished and he is willing to accept help.

3. When reviewed in the outpatient clinic 4 weeks later he is dry and denies drinking alcohol but tells you that he feels anxious and lonely at home and has constant craving to drink again.

1)   THEME: ALCOHOL RELATED PROBLEMS

Answers

1   A. Outpatient detoxification programme
         F. Motivational interviewing

2.   B. Inpatient detoxification programme
         E. Multivitamins

3.   D. Acamprosate
          H. Relapse prevention measures

Reference

Gelder, M.G., Lopez-Ibor, Jr. J.J., Andreason, N.C., (2000) *New Oxford textbook of psychiatry*, Oxford university press, pp 494-504.

2)   THEME: NEUROPHARMACOLOGY - SIDE EFFECTS

Options

    A. 5 HT 1 receptors
    B. 5 HT 2 receptors
    C. Alpha 1 Adrenergic receptors
    D. Alpha 2 Adrenergic receptors
    E. Muscaranic receptors
    F. Nicotinic receptors
    G. Dopamine receptors
    H. GABA Receptors
    I. TSH receptors
    J. H1 Histamine receptors

Select ONE option from the above list that mediates each of the following side effects described below.

1. A 32-year-old lorry driver was referred by his GP for low mood and sleep problems. Since he was started on Mirtazipine few days ago he is sleeping well but worried that he feels drowsy till late afternoon.

2. A 56-year-old lady suffering from Schizophrenia is on Depixol injection every fortnight for more than ten years and is tolerating well. In the routing follow up clinic, you notice that she makes involuntary chewing movements but not eating anything. She also repeatedly protrudes her tongue.

3. A 36-year-old lady was started on Clozapine after she failed to respond to two antipsychotics drugs. Her psychotic symptoms have improved but she is now worried that she has gained more than a stone weight in the past 6 months.

2)   THEME: NEUROPHARMACOLOGY - SIDE EFFECTS

Answers

1.   I. H1 Histamine receptors

2.   G. Dopamine receptors

3.   B. 5 HT 2 Receptors

Reference

Kendell, R.E. and Zealley, A.K. (1993) *Companion to psychiatric studies*, 5th edn. Churchill Livingstone, Edinburgh, pp261-263 & 761-762.

3)   THEME: CONCEPTS IN PSYCHOTHERAPY

Options

    A. Transference
    B. Non Verbal Thinking
    C. Natural Idiom
    D. Collective Unconscious
    E. Topographic Model
    F. Objective Psyche
    G. Archetypes
    H. Paranoid Schizoid Position
    I. Good Breast
    J. Good Enough Mother
    K. Projective identification
    L. Non interventionist

Select THREE options from the above list those are closely associated with each of the following individuals.

    1. Carl Jung.

    2. Margaret Lowenfeld.

    3. Melanie Klein.

4)   THEME: TREATMENT OF MOTOR DISORDERS

Answers

1.   B. Anticholinergics
        F. Benzodiazepines

2.   D. Haloperidol
        G. SSRI

3.   A. Cholinesterase Inhibitors
        I. Consider thymectomy

Reference

Gelder, M.G., Lopez-Ibor, Jr. J.J., Andreason, N.C., (2000) *New Oxford textbook of psychiatry,* Oxford university press, pp. 400-401, 1150 & 1323.

Lishman, W.A. (1998). *Organic psychiatry, 3rd edn.* Blackwell science, Oxford, pp. 709-710.

5)   THEME: THEORIES IN PSYCHOLOGY

Options

    A. Bowlby's theory
    B. Cannon-bard theory
    C. Erikson's theory
    D. Festinger's theory
    E. Helmholtz theory
    F. James-lange theory
    G. Kohlberg's theory
    H. Kelly's theory
    I. Lorenz theory
    J. Piaget's theory
    K. Schachter's theory

Select ONE option from the above list of theories that best describes each of the following statement.

1. Theory of attitude that claims that whenever we simultaneously hold two cognitions that are psychologically inconsistent, we experience "psychological discomfort or tension" which motivates us to reduce it by achieving consonance.

2. Theory of emotion that claims that our emotional experience is the result of perceived bodily changes.

3. Theory of development that claims that human development occurs through a genetically determined sequence of psychosocial stages, spanning the whole lifespan.

5)   THEME: THEORIES IN PSYCHOLOGY

Answers

1.   D. Festinger's theory

2.   F. James-lange theory

3.   C. Erikson's theory

Reference

Gross, R. (2001) *Psychology, the science of mind and behaviour*. 4th edition, Hodder & Stoughton. pp 361-362, 135-136 & 536.

6)   THEME: NEUROLOGICAL SIGNS

Options

   A. Ipsilateral optic atrophy
   B. Gerstman's syndrome
   C. Anosognosia
   D. Extensor plantar reflex
   E. Constructional apraxia
   F. Pseudo bulbar palsy
   G. Loss of taste sensation
   H. Nystagmus
   I. Gait ataxia

For each of the clinical scenarios given below, select TWO of the above clinical features that are most likely to be present. Each option may be used once, more than once or not at all.

1. An young girl suffering from frontal meningioma.

2. A right handed man having right parietal lobe lesion .

3. A malnourished man with chronic alcoholism.

6)   THEME: NEUROLOGICAL SIGNS

Answers

1.   A. Ipsilateral optic atrophy
       G. Loss of taste sensation

2.   C. Anosognosia
       E. Constructional apraxia

3.   H. Nystagmus
       I. Gait ataxia

Reference

Lishman, W.A. (1998). *Organic psychiatry, 3rd edn*. Blackwell science, Oxford, pp. 17-19 & 578.

7)   THEME: DIAGNOSIS OF STUPOR

Options

    A. Psychogenic stupor
    B. Manic stupor
    C. Depressive stupor
    D. Organic stupor
    E. Catatonic stupor
    F. Malingering
    G. Temporal lobe epilepsy

Select ONE option from the above list that is the most likely explanation for the following clinical situations.

1. A 40-year-old man started to feel low about four months ago when he was made redundant. He gradually became more withdrawn, lost interest in his hobbies and started losing weight. Over the past few days he completely stopped talking and virtually became immobile.

2. A 33-year-old woman is admitted to the hospital in a mute state with severe self-neglect. On examination, she is very withdrawn but awake, fully conscious yet not responding to your commands. She is holding her hand in a bizarre position for several hours.

3. A 55-year-old lady was admitted to a psychiatry unit with 2 weeks history of increasing agitation and paranoia. On examination she was very rigid, stuporous and has right papilloedema. She has no significant medical history except left mastectomy few years ago.

7)   THEME: DIAGNOSIS OF STUPOR

Answers

1.   C. Depressive stupor

2.   E. Catatonic stupor

3.   D. Organic stupor

Reference

Lishman, W.A. (1998). *Organic psychiatry, 3rd edn.* Blackwell science, Oxford, p. 155.

8)   THEME: PHENOMENOLOGY

Options

    A. Illusion
    B. Hallucination
    C. Pseudo hallucination
    D. Over valued idea
    E. Delusion
    F. Depersonalisation
    G. Derealisation
    H. De-affectualisation
    I. Anhedonia

Select ONE option from the above list of options that is best described by each of the following definitions.

1. A Perceptual experience which is figurative, not concretely real, and occurs in the inner subjective space, not in external objective space.

2. Transformation of perceptions, coming about by a mixing of the reproduced perceptions of the subject's fantasy with natural perceptions.

3. A subjective state of unreality in which there is a feeling of estrangement, either from a sense of self or from the external environment.

8)   THEME: PHENOMENOLOGY

Answers

1.   C. Pseudo hallucination

2.   A. Illusion

3.   F. Depersonalisation

Reference

Sims, A. (2003) *Symptoms in the mind, 3rd edn.* Oxford university press, pp. 96, 108 & 230.

9)   THEME: PHARMACOKINETICS

Options

    A. Undergoes extensive first pass metabolism
    B. Doesn't undergo first pass metabolism
    C. Highly soluble in lipid
    D. Actively transported across blood brain barrier
    E. Metabolised mainly by liver
    F. Can be metabolised by brain
    G. Metabolised mainly in the lungs
    H. Not metabolised in the body

Select THREE options from the above list for each of the following questions that best describe their pharmacokinetic properties. Each option may be used once, more than once or not at all.

1. Oral lithium.

2. Intravenous diazepam.

3. Oral tryptophan.

10)   THEME: MECHANISM OF ACTION OF RECEPTORS

Answers

1.   A. Adrenergic receptors
      B. Dopaminergic receptors
      D. Muscaranic receptors

2.   C. Nicotinic receptors
      E. Glycine receptors
      H. GABA A receptors

3.   F. Vitamin D receptors
      G. Thyroid hormone receptors
      I. Steroid receptors

Reference

Kendell, R.E. and Zealley, A.K. (1993) *Companion to psychiatric studies,* 5th edn. Churchill Livingstone, Edinburgh, pp. 112-118.

11)   THEME: SCHOOLS OF PSYCHOANALYTIC THEORY

Options

    A. Anna Freud
    B. Melanie Klein
    C. Margaret Mahler
    D. Erik Erikson
    E. Ronald Fairbairn
    F. Harry Guntrip
    G. Sullivan
    H. Erich Fromm
    I. Fromm-Reichmann
    J. Otto Rank
    K. Charles Brenner

Select THREE individuals from the above list who are closely associated with each of the following schools of psychoanalytic theory

1. Ego Psychology.

2. Object Relations.

3. Psychoanalytic Developmental Psychology.

11)   THEME: SCHOOLS OF PSYCHOANALYTIC THEORY

Answers

1.   A. Anna Freud
        D. Erik Erikson
        K. Charles Brenner

2.   B. Melanie Klein
        E. Ronald Fairbairn
        F. Harry Guntrip

3.   C. Margaret Mahler
        H. Erich Fromm
        J. Otto Rank

Reference

Bongar, B. & Beutler, L. E. (1995) *Comprehensive textbook of psychotherapy*, Oxford university press. pp. 38-41.

12)   THEME: MOTOR DISORDERS IN SCHIZOPHRENIA

Options

  A. Neuroleptic malignant syndrome
  B. Pernicious catatonia
  C. Manic episode
  D. Waxy flexibility
  E. Automatic obedience
  F. Negativism
  G. Echolalia
  H. Echopraxia
  I. Cataplexy
  J. Catalepsy
  K. Mitgehen

Select ONE option from the above list that best describes each of the following phenomenons seen in catatonic schizophrenia.

  1. The patient is asked to raise his right arm by the examiner. He not only raises his right arm but also raises the other arm and then stands up with both arms raised in a dramatic way.

  2. The patient imitates the interviewer's every movement of action despite him asking the patient not to.

  3. A known patient with catatonic schizophrenia was admitted under mental health act with extreme hyperactivity and disruptive behaviour. On examination she is febrile and appears very rigid. Her Blood pressure is stable and the blood investigation shows normal level of CPK levels.

13)   THEME: CONCEPTS IN ATTACHMENT

Answers

1.   C. Types of attachment
        F. Strange situation

2.   D. Contact comfort
        I. Disproved 'cup-board love' theory

3.   B. Attachment figure
        H. Maternal deprivation hypothesis

Reference

Gross, R. (1996) *Psychology, the science of mind and behaviour.* 3rd edition, Hodder & Stoughton. Pp551-561.

14)   THEME: LEARNING DISABILITY

Options

    A. Prader Willi Syndrome
    B. Williams Syndrome
    C. Angelman's Syndrome
    D. Downs Syndrome
    E. Fragile X Syndrome
    F. Von Recklinghausen's Disease
    G. Rett's Syndrome
    H. Foetal Alcohol Syndrome
    I. Edward's Syndrome
    J. Congenital rubella

Please select ONE of the above clinical syndromes, which most clearly describe the following behavioural pattern.

1. A 6-year-old boy presents with moderate learning difficulty. He was described by his parents as very social, charming and very outgoing. During the assessment you notice that he has exceptional verbal ability and fluency.

2. A 10-year-old boy with mild learning difficulty presents with Attention deficit Hyperactivity disorder like features and self-harming behaviour. On examination he has litany speech and gaze avoidance.

3. A 3-year-old girl with severe learning difficulty after a period of normal development presents with severe language and social developmental delay and abnormal midline hand wringing movements.

14)   THEME: LEARNING DISABILITY

Answers

1.   B. Williams Syndrome

2.   E. Fragile X Syndrome

3.   G. Rett's Syndrome

Reference

Gelder, M.G., Lopez-Ibor, Jr. J.J., Andreason, N.C., (2000) *New Oxford textbook of psychiatry*, Oxford university press, pp. 1954-1958.

15)   THEME: DIAGNOSIS OF COGNITIVE IMPAIRMENT

Options

    A. Delirium tremens
    B. Alzheimer's disease
    C. Vascular dementia
    D. Pick's disease
    E. Hypothyroidism
    F. Lewy body dementia
    G. Pseudo dementia
    H. Creutzfeldt-jakob disease
    I.   Subdural haematoma
    J. Parkinson's disease
    K. Korsakov's disease

Select ONE option from the above list that best describes the clinical features of each of the following clinical scenarios.

1. A 68-year-old man presents to his GP with repeated falls. On examination he has marked tremor & rigidity and moderate cognitive impairment. His wife tells the GP that he may be hallucinating as she heard him shouting when there was no one else at home.

2. A 57-year-old woman presents with 6 months history of memory loss, easy fatigueability and weight gain. Though worried about her symptoms she denies feeling depressed.

3. A 60-year-old chronic alcoholic presents with headache, memory lapses and fluctuating consciousness.

15)   THEME: DIAGNOSIS OF COGNITIVE IMPAIRMENT

Answers

1.   F. Lewy body dementia

2.   E. Hypothyroidism

3.   I. Subdural haematoma

Reference

Gelder, M.G., Lopez-Ibor, Jr. J.J., Andreason, N.C., (2000) *New Oxford textbook of psychiatry*, Oxford university press, pp 417, 440 & 1162.

16)   THEME: SIDE EFFECTS OF LITHIUM

Options

    A. Reduce the dose of lithium
    B. Increase the dose of lithium
    C. Stop lithium immediately
    D. Stop lithium and to consult the GP immediately
    E. Consider stopping lithium
    F. Check thyroid function tests
    G. Check serum lithium levels
    H. Add another mood stabiliser
    I. No action needed

Select ONE option from the above list that would be the most appropriate course of action in each of the following situation.

1. A 34 year old woman known to be suffering from Bipolar disorder well maintained on Lithium, now complaints of feeling tired, slowed down in her movements but denies feeling low. In spite of eating less she has gained more than half a stone over the past few months.

2. A 56-year-old man suffering from resistant depression was started on Lithium carbonate 600 mg as augmentation therapy in the community. Four days later he developed severe nausea, vomiting and diarrhoea. He appears tremulous and mildly unsteady. His serum lithium level is 0.76 mmol/l.

3. A 46-year-old lady was started on lithium in the ward following a hypo manic episode. During the first week she complains of feeling mildly nauseous and you notice that she has fine tremors both the hands.

16)   THEME: SIDE EFFECTS OF LITHIUM

Answers

1.   F. Check thyroid function tests

2.   D. Stop the lithium and to consult the GP immediately

3.   I. No action needed

Reference

Gelder, M.G., Lopez-Ibor, Jr. J.J., Andreason, N.C., (2000) *New Oxford textbook of psychiatry,* Oxford university press, pp. 1306-1312.

17)   THEME: SOMATOFORM DISORDERS

Options

   A. Briquet's syndrome
   B. Depressive episode
   C. Dysmorphophobia
   D. Factitious disorder
   E. Hypochondriacal disorder
   F. Malingering
   G. Munchausen's syndrome
   H. Neurasthenia
   I. Schizophrenia

Select ONE diagnosis from the above list for each of the following questions that best describes the clinical features.

1. A 27-year-old man presents anxiously to his GP requesting a referral to cosmetic surgeon for "septoplasty". He thinks his nose is "deviated and big" and people are looking at him. He even stopped going to work for the past few months. His GP didn't find any abnormality but she couldn't reassure him.

2. A 45-year-old accountant complains of feeling " exhausted" even after very minimal physical or mental effort and body aches and pain "all the time". He is anxious and frustrated that the doctors identified no physical cause but he denies feeling depressed.

3. A 37-year-old woman has been referred by her GP to various specialities for a wide range of symptoms like chest pain, weakness of legs, chronic diarrhoea and muscle pain. Usually the investigations were negative but she would demand medication to help her symptoms.

17)   THEME: SOMATOFORM DISORDERS

Answers

1.   C. Dysmorphophobia

2.   H. Neurasthenia

3.   A. Briquet's syndrome

Reference

Stein & Wilkinson (1998) *Seminars in general adult psychiatry,* Gaskell. pp 711–745.

18)   THEME: MANAGEMENT OF SIDE EFFECTS

Options

    A. Immediately stop the medication
    B. Reduce the dose and continue the medication
    C. Cautiously continue the same dose of medication
    D. Immediate admission to psychiatric ward
    E. Immediate admission to medical ward
    F. Consider referral to medical team
    G. Report immediately to General Practitioner
    H. Weekly WBC blood monitoring
    I.   Twice weekly WBC blood monitoring
    J.   Daily WBC blood monitoring
    K. Urgent blood test for Creatinine phosphokinase
    L. Steroids
    M. Cyproheptadine

Select THREE most appropriate steps from the above list of options you would consider for each of the following clinical situation. Each option may be used once, more than once or not at all.

1. A 32-year-old man known to be suffering from Schizophrenia has been on Clozapine for four months now. You receive a call from CPMS that his WBC count is 1700/ cubic mm. When you ring the patient, he tells you that he is feeling tired and lethargic for the past 2 days.

2. A 45-year-old man has been taking Fluoxetine for symptoms of low mood, reduced energy and increased appetite & weight for 3 months with no effect. On his request, Fluoxetine was stopped and two weeks later he was started on Phenelzine. Few days later, you receive a phone call from his anxious wife saying that he is very unwell, jittery and sick.

3.   A middle-aged woman suffering from resistant depression was recently started on Carbamazepine as augmentation therapy to her current medication Venlafaxine. Her mood began to improve but she is now concerned after noticing few red spots on her face. She is afebrile and appears to have small erythematous rash over her face and neck without any evidence of bleeding or exfoliation. Her white cell count is normal and she is otherwise well.

18)   THEME: MANAGEMENT OF SIDE EFFECTS

Answers

1.   A. Immediately stop the medication
        E. Immediate admission to medical ward
        J. Daily WBC blood monitoring

2.   A. Immediately stop the medication
        G. Report immediately to General Practitioner
        M. Cyproheptadine

3.   C. Cautiously continue the same dose of medication
        F. Consider referral to medical team
        L. Steroids

Reference

Schatzberg, A. F. & Nemeroff, C. B. (1998) *Textbook of psychopharmacology, 2nd edition*. American psychiatric press. pp 245, 438 & 766-767.

19)   THEME: BASIC PSYCHOPHARMACOLOGY

Options

    A. Clonidine
    B. Yohimbine
    C. Prazosin
    D. Benzodiazepines
    E. Buspirone
    F. Pindolol
    G. LSD
    H. Apomorphine
    I.   Phenylephrine
    J.   Olanzapine
    K. Paroxetine
    L. Bromocriptine
    M. Ondansetron

Select TWO options from the above list that has significant agonistic activity in the following receptors. Each option may be used once, more than once or not at all.

    1. Serotonin receptors.

    2. Dopaminergic receptors.

    3. Alpha Adrenergic receptors.

19)   THEME: BASIC PSYCHOPHARMACOLOGY

Answers

1.   E. Buspirone
        G. LSD

2.   H. Apomorphine
        L. Bromocriptine

3.   A. Clonidine
        I. Phenyephrine

Reference

Kendell, R.E. and Zealley, A.K. (1993) *Companion to psychiatric studies*, 5th edn. Churchill Livingstone, Edinburgh, pp. 127-136.

20)   THEME: HYPERACTIVITY IN CHILDREN

Options

   A. Methylphenidate
   B. Dexamphetamine
   C. Pemoline
   D. Carbamazepine
   E. Clozapine
   F. Diazepam
   G. Melatonin
   H. Reassurance only

Select ONE option from the above list that is most appropriate in the management of each of the following clinical situation.

1. A 4-year-old boy was taken to his GP by his single mom for symptoms of chest infection. She told the GP that he is 'hyper' and constantly fights with his elder brother but denies having major problems or difficulty in coping. He was described as 'very pleasant and quiet' by his reception teacher.

2. A 8-year-old boy was referred by the educational psychologist to you with gradual decline in academic performance and impulsive behaviour. He was excluded from the school twice this year for 'fighting and pushing' other pupils. Mom is 'at the end of her tether' and described him as 'full of energy' and 'always on the go'.

3. A 16-year-old teen-age boy presents with a 4 weeks history of hyperactive and irresponsible behaviour. During the interview he appears disinhibited, over confidant and tells you various fantastic stories about himself.

20)   THEME: HYPERACTIVITY IN CHILDREN

Answers

1.   H. Reassurance only

2.   A. Methylphenidate

3.   D. Carbamazepine

Reference

Goodman. R. & Scott. S., (1997). *Child psychiatry*, 1st edition. Blackwell science publications pp. 52-55 & 91.

21)   THEME: PIONEERS OF PSYCHOTHERAPY MODELS

Options

A. Adler, G
B. Bandura, A
C. Beck, A
D. Bion, W.R
E. Eysenck, H.J
F. Freud, A
G. Jung, C
II. Minuchin, S
I. Henggler
J. Rogers, C.R
K. Sullivan, H.S

Select TWO individuals from the above list of options who are closely associated with each of the following therapies.

1. Family Therapy.

2. Behaviour Therapy.

3. Group Therapy.

21)   THEME: PIONEERS OF PSYCHOTHERAPY MODELS

Answers

1.   H. Minuchin, S
        I.Henggler

2.   B. Bandura, A
        E. Eysenck, H.J

3.   D. Bion, W.R
        K. Sullivan, H.S

Reference

Bongar, B. & Beutler, L. E. (1995) *Comprehensive textbook of psychotherapy*, Oxford university press. pp. 347-349, 71-72, 182 & 191.

22)   THEME: CONCEPTS IN THOUGHT DISORDER

Options

   A. Over inclusive thinking
   B. Loosening of associations
   C. Thought insertion
   D. Thought echo
   E. Concrete thinking
   F. Thought block
   G. Determining tendency
   H. Derailment
   I. Asyndesis
   J. Fusion
   K. Preservation
   L. Constellation

Select TWO options from the above list of psychopathological concepts for each of the following individuals with whom they are closely associated. Each option may be used once, more than once or not at all.

1. Carl Schneider.

2. Cameron.

3. Jaspers.

22)   THEME: CONCEPTS IN THOUGHT DISORDER

Answers

1.   H. Derailment
      J. Fusion

2.   A. Over inclusive thinking
      I. Asyndesis

3.   G. Determining tendency
      L. Constellation

Reference

Sims, A. (2003) *Symptoms in the mind, 3rd edn*. Oxford university press, pp. 151-160.

23)   THEME: ATTACHMENT STYLES

Options

    A. Anxious attachment behaviour
    B. Avoidant attachment behaviour
    C. Borderline attachment behaviour
    D. Disorganised attachment behaviour
    E. Secure attachment behaviour
    F. Sensitive attachment behaviour

Select ONE option from the above list for each of the following attachment style described below.

1. Baby is indifferent to mother's presence. Minimal or no distress when she leaves and ignores when she returns. Can be comforted as easily by the stranger as by the mother.

2. Baby plays happily in mother's presence. Distressed when she leaves and seeks immediate contact when she returns. Quickly calms down and resumes play.

3. Baby is fussy and wary in mother's presence. Very distressed when she leaves and seeks contact when she returns but also angry and resists contact. Doesn't return to play readily.

23)   THEME: ATTACHMENT STYLES

Answers

1.   B. Avoidant attachment behaviour

2.   E. Secure attachment behaviour

3.   A. Anxious attachment behaviour

Reference

Gross, R. (2001) *Psychology, the science of mind and behaviour.*4th edition, Hodder & Stoughton. pp 463-465.

24)   THEME: LEARNING DISABILITY

Options

   A. Prader Willi Syndrome
   B. Williams Syndrome
   C. Angelman's Syndrome
   D. Downs Syndrome
   E. Fragile X Syndrome
   F. Von Recklinghausen's Disease
   G. Rett's Syndrome
   H. Edward's Syndrome
   I. Congenital rubella
   J. Lesch-Nyhan Syndrome
   K. Foetal Alcohol Syndrome
   L. Klinefelter's Syndrome

Select ONE of the above clinical syndromes, which most clearly describe the following behavioural pattern.

1. An 8 year old boy was taken to his GP by her ex-publican mother that he is 'always on the go' and poor academic performance. On examination he has mild growth retardation, short palpebral fissure and hypertelorism.

2. A young boy with severe learning difficulties and choreo athetosis presents with serious self-mutilating behaviour.

3. A young boy with moderate learning difficulty was described by his parents as very placid, outgoing and socially responsive.

24)   THEME: LEARNING DISABILITY

Answers

1.   K. Foetal Alcohol Syndrome

2.   J. Lesch-Nyhan Syndrome

3.   D. Downs Syndrome

Reference

Gelder, M.G., Lopez-Ibor, Jr. J.J., Andreason, N.C., (2000) *New Oxford textbook of psychiatry*, Oxford university press, pp. 1954-1960.

25)   THEME: COGNITIVE IMPAIRMENT - TREATMENT

Options

  A. Antidepressant trial
  B. Anticholinergics
  C. Antipsychotics
  D. Dopaminergic agents
  E. Thyroid hormone supplements
  F. Cholinesterase inhibitors
  G. Supportive therapy only
  H. No treatment needed

Select ONE option from the above list that is the most appropriate treatment option for each of the following clinical situation with cognitive impairment.

  1. A 60-year-old present with rapidly progressive memory loss of 4 weeks duration. On examination he appears very stiff and unsteady on his feet. He has bilateral myoclonic jerks with extensor plantar reflexes.

  2. A 69-year-old previously fit and healthy woman presents with increasing forgetfulness over the past two years and difficulty in recognizing and naming objects. On minimental state examination she scored 23/30.

  3. A 66-year-old lady presents with increasing forgetfulness, loss of interest and loss of weight since the death of her husband about 4 months ago. She scored 21 on minimental examination, but answered 'don't know' for several questions.

25)   THEME: COGNITIVE IMPAIRMENT – TREATMENT

Answers

1.   G. Supportive therapy only

2.   F. Cholinesterase inhibitors

3.   A. Antidepressant trial

Reference

Gelder, M.G., Lopez-Ibor, Jr. J.J., Andreason, N.C., (2000) *New Oxford textbook of psychiatry*, Oxford university press, pp. 393-395, 412 & 693.

26)   THEME: EEG FINDINGS

Options

    A. Increase in alpha activity
    B. Loss of alpha rhythm
    C. Triphasic sharp wave complexes at 1-2 Hz
    D. Widespread theta activity
    E. Periodic spike and slow wave activity over temporal lobes
    F. Generalised spike and slow wave activity

Select ONE option from the above list of EEG findings which is more likely to be present in each of the following clinical situation

1. A 57-year-old woman presents with progressive short-term memory loss, personality change and myoclonic jerks. Her CT scan shows mild cortical atrophy.

2. A 34-year lady presented to A&E with headache, high fever and drowsiness. On examination she appeared very confused, rigid with asymmetric reflexes. CT scan ruled out cerebral abscess and space occupying lesion.

3. A 46-year-old woman presented with repeated falls and clumsiness. Her family has noticed that she has become more forgetful recently and generally morose and quarrelsome.

26)   THEME: EEG FINDINGS

Answers

1.   C. Triphasic sharp wave complexes at 1-2 Hz. (Creutzfeldt-Jakob disease)

2.   E. Periodic spike and slow wave activity over temporal lobes. (Herpes Simplex Encephalitis)

3.   B. Loss of alpha rhythm. (Huntington's Disease)

Reference

Lishman, W.A. (1998). *Organic psychiatry, 3rd edn.* Blackwell science, Oxford, pp. 357& 465- 479.

27)   THEME: TREATMENT OF ANXIETY DISORDERS

Options

   A. Reassurance and education
   B. Cognitive behaviour therapy
   C. Psychodynamic psychotherapy
   D. Exposure and response prevention
   E. Anxiety management training
   F. Long acting benzodiazepines
   G. Short acting benzodiazepines
   H. Antidepressants
   I. No treatment needed

Select TWO options from the above list that you consider more appropriate in the management of the following clinical situations. Each option can be used once, more than once or not at all.

   1. A 24-year-old man presents with recurrent episodes of intense anxiety without any obvious precipitant over the past few weeks and he is currently off sick from work. During those episodes he feels shaky and tremulous with chest discomfort. No physical cause was found.

   2. A 32-year-old phlebotomist presents with constant worry & tension and difficulty to relax for the past few weeks. She also complains of palpitation and dizziness but denies having any panic attacks or phobia to any particular situation. She denies feeling low and continues to work without major difficulties.

   3. A 45-year-old businessman has dental carries and is due to attend the clinic for dental extraction in 3 weeks time. He already cancelled the appointment twice and worries all the time. His wife now convinced him to see a mental health professional for help.

27)   THEME: TREATMENT OF ANXIETY DISORDERS

Answers

1.   B. Cognitive behaviour therapy
      F. Long acting benzodiazepines

2.   A. Reassurance and education
      E. Anxiety management training

3.   D. Exposure and response prevention
      E. Anxiety management training

Reference

Gelder, M., Gath, D., Mayou, R., and Cowen, P., (1996) *Oxford textbook of psychiatry, 3rd edition.* Oxford university press, pp. 161–180.

28)   THEME: POST PARTUM MENTAL DISORDERS

Options

- A. Consider starting an antidepressant medication
- B. Consider antipsychotics medication
- C. Few weeks supply of Benzodiazepines only
- D. No drug treatment necessary
- E. Consider Cognitive Behaviour therapy
- F. Electro convulsive therapy
- G. Immediate detention under mental health act
- H. Consider admission to mother and baby unit
- I. Reassurance only

Select TWO options from the above list that are more appropriate in the management of each of the following postpartum situations. Each option may be used once, more than once or not at all.

1. A 32-year-old lady presents to her GP with symptoms of low mood for the past two months. She lost interest in her hobbies and lost half a stone of weight. She denies any self harm ideas or hostile feelings towards her 5 months old baby.

2. A 30-year-old lady with no past psychiatric history gave birth to a healthy full term baby by caesarean section. A week later, she suddenly became very disruptive in the ward, singing and dancing with joy, telling everyone that her baby is "The lord". She stays awake all night in the ward and inconsiderate of others, which is not her usual self.

3. A 23-year-old primigravida is observed to be intermittently tearful and irritable by the obstetrics ward nurse few days after her delivery. She denies feeling low though her mood tends to fluctuate.

28)   THEME: POST PARTUM MENTAL DISORDERS

Answers

1.   A. Consider starting an antidepressant medication
      E. Consider Cognitive Behaviour therapy

2.   F. Electro convulsive therapy
      H. Consider admission to mother and baby unit

3.   D. No drug treatment necessary
      I. Reassurance only

Reference

Gelder, M., Gath, D., Mayou, R., and Cowen, P., (1996) *Oxford textbook of psychiatry, 3rd edition.* Oxford university press, pp. 395-397.

29)   THEME: PRESCRIPTION IN PREGNANCY

Options

    A. Few weeks supply of Diazepam
    B. Gradually stop the current medication and start on Chlorpromazine
    C. Promethazine
    D. Citalopram
    E. Amitriptyline
    F. Venlafaxine
    G. Change to Clopixol depot injection
    H. Add folic acid and continue the current treatment
    I. Gradually stop Lithium and monitor mental state
    J. No drug treatment necessary

Select ONE appropriate step from the above list of options for each of the following clinical situation.

1. A 28-year-old young woman came back from holiday and was very upset when she found out that her house was broken into. A week later she presents to her GP with severe insomnia and anxiety and requests some medication to 'calm' her down. She is 8 weeks pregnant and her GP doesn't think she is depressed.

2. A 32-year-old young lady known to be suffering from schizophrenia for several years tells you that she is currently in a relationship and quite keen to have a baby. She has been on Risperidone for 4 years now.

3. A 31-year-old lady had a hypmanic episode 2 years ago and since then she is on Lithium with no relapse. She wants to become pregnant and wants your advice regarding medication.

29)   THEME: PRESCRIPTION IN PREGNANCY

Answers

1.   C. Promethazine

2.   B. Gradually stop the current medication and start on Chlorpromazine

3.   I. Gradually stop Lithium and monitor mental state

Reference

Schatzberg, A. F. & Nemeroff, C. B. (1998) *Textbook of psychopharmacology, 2nd edition*. American psychiatric press. pp. 982-990.

30)   THEME: SEX PATTERN IN MENTAL ILLNESS

Options

  A. Autistic disorders
  B. Deliberate self-harm
  C. Hyperactivity disorders
  D. Prepubertal depression
  E. Postpubertal depression
  F. School refusal
  G. Selective mutism
  H. Specific phobias
  I. Tic disorders

Select THREE options from the above list for each of the following sex incidence pattern described below.

  1. More common in girls.

  2. More common in boys.

  3. Equal incidence in both sexes.

30)   THEME: SEX PATTERN IN MENTAL ILLNESS

Answers

1.   B. Deliberate self-harm
        E. Postpubertal depression
        H. Specific phobias

2.   A. Autistic disorders
        C. Hyperactivity disorders
        I. Tic disorders

3.   D. Prepubertal depression
        F. School refusal
        G. Selective mutism

Reference:

Goodman. R & Scott. S., (1997). *Child psychiatry*, 1st edition. Blackwell science publications, p 36.

31)   THEME: MANAGEMENT OF DRUG MISUSE

Options

    A. High doses of diazepam
    B. Heroin replacement
    C. Methadone replacement
    D. Relapse prevention measures
    E. Buprenorphine
    F. Naltrexone
    G. Naloxone
    H. No treatment necessary

Select ONE option from the above list for each of the following questions that are more appropriate in the management of this patient. Each option may be used once, more than once or not at all.

1. A 30-year-old ex-heroin user has been maintained on Methadone for the past 6 years. His dose has been gradually reduced to 30 mg/day. He is now complaining of increasing withdrawal effects and has been admitted for in-patient detoxification.

2. Three days after admission he was found collapsed on the floor in his room by the nursing staff. On examination his GCS is 5 and pupils are constricted. His pulse rate is 88/min, BP 110/70 mm Hg and respiratory rate is 6/min.

3. When reviewed in the follow up clinic, a week after discharge, he tells you that he doesn't use heroin but occasionally craves for it.

31)   THEME: MANAGEMENT OF DRUG MISUSE

Answers

1.   E. Buprenorphine

2.   G. Naloxone

3.   D. Relapse prevention measures

Reference

Gelder, M.G., Lopez-Ibor, Jr. J.J., Andreason, N.C., (2000) *New Oxford textbook of psychiatry,* Oxford university press, pp 523-531.

32)   THEME: PSYCHOLOGICAL THERAPIES

Options

- A. Hypnosis
- B. Free association
- C. Transference
- D. Highly structured interviews
- E. Negative automatic thoughts
- F. Reciprocal role procedure
- G. Diary keeping
- H. Circular questioning
- I.   Reformulation letter
- J.   Dream interpretation
- K. Character armour
- L. Good-bye letter

Select THREE options from the above list that characterises each of the following therapies.

1. Cognitive Behaviour Therapy.

2. Cognitive Analytic Therapy.

3. Psychoanalytic Psychotherapy.

32)   THEME: PSYCHOLOGICAL THERAPIES

Answers

1.   D. Highly structured interviews
      E. Negative automatic thoughts
      G. Diary keeping

2.   F. Reciprocal role procedure
      I. Reformulation letter
      L. Good-bye letter

3.   B. Free association
      C. Transference
      J. Dream interpretation

Reference

Bongar, B. & Beutler, L. E. (1995) *Comprehensive textbook of psychotherapy*, Oxford university press. pp. 161-165 & 25-28.

Clarkson, P. & Pokorny, M. (1994) *Handbook of psychotherapy.* Routleget p.222.

33)   THEME: PHENOMENOLOGY IN ILLNESS

Options

    A. Paranoid schizophrenia
    B. Simple schizophrenia
    C. Hypochondriasis
    D. Delirium tremens
    E. Viral encephalitis
    F. Psychotic depression
    G. Manic episode
    H. Anorexia nervosa
    I. Temporal lobe epilepsy
    J. Morbid jealousy
    K. Acute stress reaction
    L. Panic disorder

Select THREE conditions from the above list of options that are more likely to have the following psychopathology.

1. Delusion.

2. Overvalued idea.

3. Visual hallucination.

33)   THEME: PHENOMENOLOGY IN ILLNESS

Answers

1.   A. Paranoid schizophrenia
        F. Psychotic depression
        G. Manic episode

2.   C. Hypochondriasis
        H. Anorexia nervosa
        J. Morbid jealousy

3.   D. Delirium tremens
        E. Viral encephalitis
        I. Temporal lobe epilepsy

Reference

Sims, A. (2003) *Symptoms in the mind, 3rd edn*. Oxford university press, pp. 102-105 & 143-144.

34)   THEME: GENETIC DISORDERS

Options

    A. Prader Willi Syndrome
    B. Williams Syndrome
    C. Angelman's Syndrome
    D. Downs Syndrome
    E. Fragile X Syndrome
    F. Von Recklinghausen's Disease
    G. Rett's Syndrome
    H. Edward's Syndrome
    I. Cri-Du-Chat Syndrome
    J. Klinefelter's Syndrome
    K. Turner's Syndrome
    L. Lesch-Nyhan Syndrome

Select ONE of the above clinical syndromes that most clearly describes the following clinical phenotype.

1. A 17-year-old short young girl presents with primary amenorrhoea. On examination she has short webbed neck, cubitus valgus with poor development of secondary sexual characteristics.

2. A young man with learning difficulty has long facial contour with large jaw and macro orchadism.

3. One-year-old boy presents with failure to thrive and feeding difficulties to the paediatrician. On examination he observed elfin like face with wide mouth and systolic heart murmur.

34)   THEME: GENETIC DISORDERS

Answers

1.   K. Turner's Syndrome

2.   E. Fragile X Syndrome

3.   B. Williams Syndrome

Reference

Gelder, M.G., Lopez-Ibor, Jr. J.J., Andreason, N.C., (2000) *New Oxford textbook of psychiatry,* Oxford university press, pp. 1954-1960.

Lishman, W.A. (1998). *Organic psychiatry, 3rd edn.* Blackwell science, Oxford, pp. 527-528.

35)   THEME: TREATMENT OF EPILEPSY

Options

  A. Acetazolamide
  B. Carbamazepine
  C. Clonazepam
  D. Diazepam
  E. Ethosuximide
  F. Gabapentin
  G. Phenobarbitone
  H. Phenytoin
  I. Sodium Valproate

For each of the following type of epilepsy, Select ONE option from the above list of medications. Each option can be used once, more than once or not at all.

1. A 17-year-old boy while drinking coffee, suddenly twists his neck, flung his arm violently and dropped the cup. He can have up to several similar attacks a day and he is known to be suffering from absence attacks.

2. A 34-year-old woman complains that she frequently smells "burnt rubber" in the ward. She appears to be fully oriented and conscious and an EEG taken during the experience shows rhythmic spike and sharp waves.

3. A middle-aged man suffering from schizophrenia suddenly lost consciousness and fell down to the floor. He then violently shook all parts of his body for a minute and fell asleep. When he woke up after a couple of hours later, he appears drowsy and complains of headache. He is regularly taking Clozapine and his WBC count is within normal limits.

35)   THEME: TREATMENT OF EPILEPSY

Answers

1.   I. Sodium Valproate

2.   B. Carbamazepine

3.   H. Phenytoin

Reference

Lishman, W.A. (1998). *Organic psychiatry, 3rd edn*. Blackwell science, Oxford, pp. 300-305.

36)   THEME: DISORDERS OF MEMORY

Options

    A. Korsakov syndrome
    B. Delirium tremens
    C. Alcoholic hallucinosis
    D. Paranoid schizophrenia
    E. Manic episode
    F. Dementia
    G. Pseudo dementia
    H. Cotard's syndrome
    I. Ganser syndrome
    J. Malingering

Select ONE option from the above list of illnesses that best describes each of the following situations with memory disturbances.

1. A 68-year-old lady was brought to the GP surgery by her son for increasing forgetfulness of 4 months duration. During the interview she appears dull, apathic and withdrawn. She scored only 21 in the mini mental scale of cognitive assessment but answered 'don't know' for many questions.

2. A 58-year-old man with chronic alcohol related problems was admitted to the ward for detoxification programme. Few days later, he elaborates enthusiastically how he spent the previous day in Edinburgh festival with his wife. But the nursing staff inform you that he hasn't left the ward since admission.

3. A young female prisoner suddenly complains of paralysis of her left leg, but no physical cause was found. During the assessment she gives approximate answers and looks mildly confused.

36)   THEME: DISORDERS OF MEMORY

Answers

1.   G. Pseudo dementia

2.   A. Korsakov syndrome

3.   I. Ganser syndromes

Reference

Sims, A. (2003) *Symptoms in the mind, 3rd edn*. Oxford university press, pp. 67-76.

37)   THEME: PERSONALITY DISORDERS

Options

    A. Anankastic personality disorder
    B. Cyclothymic personality disorder
    C. Dependent personality disorder
    D. Depressive personality disorder
    E. Histrionic personality disorder
    F. Schizoid personality disorder
    G. Schizotypal personality disorder

Select ONE option from the above list of personality disorders that best describes each of the following individuals.

1. A 34-year-old woman and her husband were referred to marital therapy. He describes her as "vain, inconsiderate and demanding" and complains that she emotionally blackmails him. During the interview she was initially upset and tearful, but soon became animated & joyful and she generally appeared quite dramatic and shallow in her feelings.

2. A 17-year-old boy is brought to his GP by his mother who thinks he is "odd". She describes him as aloof, detached and emotionally cold for a "long time". He doesn't have any friends and spends most of the time on his own "in a fantasy world". His hobbies are fishing and collecting stamps.

3. A 46-year-old unemployed man approached his GP with low mood and difficulty in coping with life since he lost his wife about 3 years ago of breast cancer. He described her as "dynamic, energetic" who made most of the decisions. His daughter described him as "always weak-willed, unduly compliant and lack vigour".

37)   THEME: PERSONALITY DISORDERS

Answers

1.   E. Histrionic personality disorder

2.   F. Schizoid personality disorder

3.   C. Dependent personality disorder

Reference

Gelder, M., Gath, D., Mayou, R., and Cowen, P., (1996) *Oxford textbook of psychiatry, 3rd edition*. Oxford university press, pp. 112-118.

38)   THEME: SERIOUS SIDE EFFECTS OF MEDICATIONS

Options

    A. Carbamezepine
    B. Phenelzine
    C. Zuclopenthixol
    D. Carbamazepine
    E. Clozapine
    F. Sodium valproate
    G. Lithium
    H. Fluoxetine

Select the most likely medication from the above list that causes each of the following uncommon, but serious side effects.

1. A 35-year-old man known to be suffering from Schizoaffective illness for several years is on regular oral antipsychotics medication for 6 months now. He presents to his GP with fever, malaise and sore throat. His WBC count is 2200/cubic mm.

2. A 34-year-old lady suffering from rheumatoid arthritis started to feel low few months ago and was started on a new medication in addition to Venlafaxine as augmentation therapy. Few weeks later, his CPN is ringing you anxiously saying that the patient is feeling very unwell, sick, unsteady on his feet and very tremulous.

3. A 45-year-old man developed low mood, increased appetite and weight gain. He was diagnosed as suffering from atypical depression and was treated with Tranylcypramine for several months with no effect. After his specific request, you stopped it and a week later prescribed him a new antidepressant. You receive a phone call from his anxious wife few days later saying that he is very unwell, jittery and sick.

38)   THEME: SERIOUS SIDE EFFECTS OF MEDICATIONS

Answers

1.   E. Clozapine

2.   G. Lithium

3.   H. Fluoxetine

Reference

Schatzberg, A. F. & Nemeroff, C. B. (1998) *Textbook of psychopharmacology, 2nd edition*. American psychiatric press. pp 766-767, 403-404 & 245.

39)   THEME: CONTROLLED DRUGS

Options

    A. Anabolic steroids
    B. Cannabis
    C. Paracetamol
    D. Morphine
    E. Lysergic Acid
    F. Barbiturates
    G. Diazepam
    H. Heroin
    I. Pholcodine
    J. Mazindol
    K. Buspirone

Select three options from the above list for each class of controlled drugs described below.

1. Class A.

2. Class B.

3. Class C.

39)   THEME: CONTROLLED DRUGS

Answers

1.   D. Morphine
      E. Lysergic Acid
      H. Heroin

2.   B. Cannabis
      F. Barbiturates
      I. Pholcodine

3.   A. Anabolic steroids
      G. Diazepam
      J. Mazindol

Reference

British National Formulary.

40)   THEME: DIAGNOSIS OF HYPERACTIVITY

Options

    A. Autism
    B. Attention Deficit Hyperactivity Disorder
    C. Depressive episode
    D. Situational hyperactivity
    E. Hypo manic episode
    F. Schizophrenia
    G. Conduct disorder
    H. Asperger's syndrome

For each of the following clinical description, select ONE diagnosis from the above list of options.

1. A 9-year-old boy was referred by his GP for 'hyperactive and disrespectful behaviour' for the past few months since her mom's new partner moved in to live with them. In the clinic while she was describing the problems, he was listening attentively to her and he didn't appear fidgety. He has high grades in studies and has no problems at school.

2. A 14-year-old boy was referred by the social service for 'fire setting and dangerous behaviour'. His mum described him as 'defiant, aggressive and disrespectful'. He has started using cannabis recently and school has significant problems in managing his behaviour.

3. A 7-year-old boy was referred by his GP, as his parents couldn't cope and 'he is a hard work'. During the assessment he appeared restless, lost interest in the various toys within few minutes and he was constantly trying to climb the windows and chairs.

**40)	THEME:	DIAGNOSIS OF HYPERACTIVITY**

Answers

1.	D. Situational hyperactivity

2.	G. Conduct disorder

3.	B. Attention Deficit Hyperactivity Disorder

Reference:

Goodman. R. & Scott. S., (1997). *Child psychiatry*, 1st edition. Blackwell science publications pp 50 – 57.

41)   THEME: DSM IV DIAGNOSTIC CRITERIA

Options

A. Symptoms for minimum of one-week duration
B. Symptoms for minimum of two weeks duration
C. Symptoms for minimum of one-month duration
D. Symptoms for minimum of one year duration
E. Social withdrawal
F. Psychomotor retardation
G. Psychomotor agitation
H. Flight of ideas
I. Self harm ideas
J. Second person auditory hallucinations
K. Third person auditory hallucinations
L. Visual hallucinations

Select THREE criteria from the above list those are included in the diagnostic criteria of each of the following illness according to Diagnostic and Statistical Manual of Mental Disorders IV. Each option may be used once, more than once or not at all.

1. Simple schizophrenia.

2. Major Depressive episode.

3. Manic episode.

41)   THEME: DSM IV DIAGNOSTIC CRITERIA

Answers

1.   D. Symptoms for minimum of one-year duration
       E. Social withdrawal
       F. Psychomotor retardation

2.   B. Symptoms for minimum of two weeks duration
       F. Psychomotor retardation
       I. Self harm ideas

3.   A. Symptoms for minimum of one-week duration
       G. Psychomotor agitation
       H. Flight of ideas

Reference:

Diagnostic and Statistical Manual of Mental Disorders. Fourth edition. Washington D.C, American psychiatric association, 1994.

42)   THEME: CONCEPTS IN PSYCHOTHERAPY

Options

    J. Transference
    K. Objective countertransference
    L. Psychodrama
    M. Transitional object
    N. Cathartic model
    O. Instinctual drives
    P. Good enough mother
    Q. Role reversal and protagonist
    R. Attachment theory
    S. Spontaneity-creativity theory

Select THREE options from the above list those are closely associated with each of the following individuals.

1. Sigmund Freud.

2. Donald Winnicott.

3. Jacob L. Moreno.

42)   THEME: CONCEPTS IN PSYCHOTHERAPY

Answers

1.   A. Transference
        E. Cathartic Model
        F. Instinctual Drives

2.   B. Objective Countertransference
        D. Transitional Object
        G. Good Enough Mother

3.   C. Psychodrama
        H. Role Reversal And Protagonist
        J. Spontaneity-Creativity Theory

Reference

Bongar, B. & Beutler, L. E. (1995) *Comprehensive textbook of psychotherapy*, Oxford university press. pp. 24-37.

Brown, D. & Pedder, J. (1991) *Introduction to psychotherapy*, 2nd edition, Routledge. Pp. 106-108 & 169-170.

43)   THEME: AETIOLOGY OF LOW MOOD

Options

A. Family history of schizophrenia
B. Family history of depression
C. Family history of diabetes
D. Loss of mother in early childhood
E. Recent life event
F. Emotional or sexual abuse in the past
G. Presence of 2 or more school age children at home
H. Amphetamine use

Select TWO options from the above list for each of the following questions that are more likely to be etiologically associated. Each option may be used once, more than once or not at all.

1. A 35-year-old successful bank manager present with 3 months history of low mood that "came out of the blue".

2. A 21-year-old man was admitted to psychiatric ward in a very agitated state under mental health act. He believes that "people are out there" to get him and they have been following him for the past 3 weeks. He also accuses the nursing staff of poisoning him and refuses to eat the food provided in the ward.

3. A 34-year-old single mother presents with difficulty in coping with life and excessive worries. She has been sleeping poorly and lost about half a stone of weight.

43)   THEME: AETIOLOGY OF LOW MOOD

Answers

1.   B. Family history of depression
       D. Loss of mother in early childhood

2.   A. Family history of schizophrenia
       H. Amphetamine use

3.   E. Recent life event
       G. Presence of 2 or more school age children at home

Reference

Gelder, M., Gath, D., Mayou, R., and Cowen, P., (1996) *Oxford textbook of psychiatry, 3rd edition*. Oxford university press, pp. 213-219 & 473-474.

44)   THEME: PSYCHOPATHOLOGY

Options

    A. Second person auditory hallucinations
    B. Third person auditory hallucinations
    C. Tactile hallucinations
    D. Poverty of speech
    E. Chronic disorganised thought process
    F. Psychomotor retardation
    G. Marked excitability
    H. Insidious development of odd behaviour
    I. Severe motor restlessness
    J. Social withdrawal
    K. Thought insertion

Select THREE options from the above list, which are more likely to be present in each of the following clinical conditions. Each option may be used once, more than once or not at all.

1. Simple schizophrenia.

2. Psychotic depression.

3. Delirium tremens.

44)   THEME: PSYCHOPATHOLOGY

Answers

1.   E. Chronic disorganised thought process
      H. Insidious development of odd behaviour
      J. Social withdrawal

2.   A. Second person auditory hallucinations
      F. Psychomotor retardation
      J. Social withdrawal

3.   C. Tactile hallucinations
      G. Marked excitability
      I. Severe motor restlessness

Reference

Sims, A. (2003) *Symptoms in the mind, 3rd edn.* Oxford university press, pp. 45 & 163.

Gelder, M.G., Lopez-Ibor, Jr. J.J., Andreason, N.C., (2000) *New Oxford textbook of psychiatry,* Oxford university press, pp. 282-283.

45)   THEME: THEORIES OF PERSONALITY

Options

    A. Orthogonal method of factor analysis
    B. Oblique method of factor analysis
    C. Idiographic approach
    D. Psychodynamic approach
    E. Neuroticism Vs Psychoticism
    F. Introversion Vs Extroversion
    G. Several source traits
    H. Repertory grid
    I. 16-personality factor questionnaire
    J. Maudsley personality inventory
    K. Useful in formal thought disorder
    L. Useful in diagnosing personality disorder

Select THREE options from the above list for each of the following approach with which they are closely associated.

1. Eysenck's hierarchical model.

2. Cattell's trait theory.

3. Kelly's personal construct theory.

45)   THEME: THEORIES OF PERSONALITY

Answers

1.   A. Orthogonal method of factor analysis
        F. Introversion Vs Extroversion
        J. Maudsley personality inventory

2.   B. Oblique method of factor analysis
        G. Several source traits
        I. 16-personality factor questionnaire

3.   C. Idiographic approach
        H. Repertory grid
        K. Useful in formal thought disorder

Reference

Gross, R. (2001) *Psychology, the science of mind and behaviour.* 4th edition, Hodder & Stoughton. pp 610-621.

46)   THEME: NEURO PATHOLOGICAL FINDINGS

Options

    A. Lateral ventricular enlargement
    B. Haemorrhagic lesions in Mamilliary bodies
    C. Lesions in Medial dorsal nucleus of thalamus
    D. Increased volume of hippocampus
    E. Decreased volume of caudate nucleus
    F. Increased activity in orbitofrontal cortex
    G. Widespread reduction in grey matter
    H. Spino bulbar degeneration
    I. Aqueduct stenosis

Select TWO pathological findings from the above list for each of the following mental illness with which they are commonly associated. Each option may be used once, more than once or not at all.

1. Obsessive-compulsive disorder.

2. Schizophrenia.

3. Korsakov's syndrome.

46)   THEME: NEURO PATHOLOGICAL FINDINGS

Answers

1.   E. Decreased volume of caudate nucleus
       F. Increased activity in orbitofrontal cortex

2.   A. Lateral ventricular enlargement
       G. Widespread reduction in grey matter

3.   B. Haemorrhagic lesions in Mamilliary bodies
       C. Lesions in Medial dorsal nucleus of thalamus

Reference

Kaplan, H.I and Sadock, B.J. (1995) *Comprehensive Textbook Of Psychiatry,*. Williams & Wilkins, pp. 915 – 917, 1219 & 269 -270.

47)   THEME: ASSESSMENT TOOLS

Options

    A. CAGE questionnare
    B. POMS
    C. GHQ 12
    D. Becks depression inventory
    E. BPRS
    F. MADRS
    G. WAIS
    H. MMSE
    I. Diagnostic Interview schedule
    J. Present state examination

Select ONE option from the above list that is very useful in the following situation

1. Self-filling screening tool for psychiatric 'caseness'.

2. To assess the severity of depression.

3. Alcohol screening.

47)   THEME: ASSESSMENT TOOLS

Answers

1.   C. GHQ 12

2.   F. MADRS

3.   A. CAGE questionnare

Reference

Kaplan, H.I and Sadock, B.J. (1995) *Comprehensive Textbook Of Psychiatry, volume I.* Williams & Wilkins, pp. 619-623.

48)   THEME: INVESTIGATION OF LOW MOOD

Options

    A. Liver function tests
    B. Renal function test
    C. Thyroid function tests
    D. Urinary cortisol estimation
    E. Sex hormone assay
    F. Serum growth hormone assay
    G. Random blood glucose
    H. Ultrasound abdomen
    I. Echocardiogram
    J. Bone marrow biopsy

Select ONE option from the above list for each of the following situation that you consider the most appropriate investigation.

1. An 18-year-old young man presents with two months history of low mood, weight loss despite "eating too much". He also complains that his sleep is very disturbed because he has to empty his bladder several times a night.

2. A 36-year-old woman presents with low mood, tiredness and weight gain. On examination she has several purple striae over her abdomen and mild hirsutism. Her BP is 160/122 mm Hg.

3. A 45-year-old woman present to her GP with easy fatigueability, low mood and cold intolerance. She has gained more than a stone weight despite poor appetite and eating less.

48)   THEME: INVESTIGATION OF LOW MOOD

Answers

1.   G. Random blood glucose

2.   D. Urinary cortisol estimation

3.   C. Thyroid function tests

Reference

Gelder, M., Gath, D., Mayou, R., and Cowen, P., (1996) *Oxford textbook of psychiatry, 3rd edition*. Oxford university press, pp. 403- 406.

49)   THEME: PHARMACOKINETICS

Option

A. Useful in emergency situations
B. Doesn't cross blood brain barrier
C. May undergo extensive first pass metabolism
D. Doesn't undergo hepatic metabolism
E. Useful in administering irritating drugs
F. Free from side effects
G. Safe and convenient to use
H. Contraindicated in anticoagulant therapy
I. Not useful for oily preparations
J. Increases the volume of distribution

Select TWO pharmacokinetic properties from the above list of options for each of the following route of administration of drugs.

1. Oral route of administration.

2. Intra muscular route of administration.

3. Intravenous route of administration.

49)   THEME: PHARMACOKINETICS

Answers

1.   C. May undergo extensive first pass metabolism
       G. Safe and convenient to use

2.   E. Useful in administering irritating drugs
       H. Contraindicated in anticoagulant therapy

3.   A. Useful in emergency situations
       I. Not useful for oily preparations

Reference

Kendell, R.E. and Zealley, A.K. (1993) *Companion to psychiatric studies*, 5th edn. Churchill Livingstone, Edinburgh, p. 106.

50)   THEME: AETIOLOGY OF MENTAL RETARDATION

Options

K. Prader Willi Syndrome
L. Lesch-Nyhan Syndrome
M. Othello syndrome
N. Angelman's Syndrome
O. Fragile X Syndrome
P. Neurofibromatosis
Q. Rett's Syndrome
R. Williams Syndrome
S. Foetal Alcohol Syndrome
T. Klinefelter's Syndrome
U. Downs Syndrome
V. Cri-Du-Chat Syndrome

Select TWO causes from the above list that commonly presents with following range of severity of mental retardation.

1. Low normal to normal IQ.

2. Mild to moderate mental retardation.

3. Severe to profound mental retardation.

50)   THEME: AETIOLOGY OF MENTAL RETARDATION

Answers

1.   F. Neurofibromatosis
        J. Klinefelter's Syndrome

2.   A. Prader Willi Syndrome
        E. Fragile X Syndrome

3.   D. Angelman's Syndrome
        G. Rett's Syndrome

Reference

Gelder, M.G., Lopez-Ibor, Jr. J.J., Andreason, N.C., (2000) *New Oxford textbook of psychiatry*, Oxford university press, pp. 1053-1061.

51)   THEME: EFFECTS OF DRUGS

Options

    A. Barbiturates
    B. Heroin
    C. Cocaine
    D. Amphetamine
    E. LSD
    F. MDMA
    G. Cannabis
    H. Glue
    I. Alcohol
    J. Nicotine

Select ONE option from the above list of drugs for each of the following questions that best describes the clinical features of the drug use.

1. Characterised by progressive modulations of sensory, usually visual, imagery generated both from external objects and distortions of eidetic imagery. Pupils are dilated with signs of autonomic arousal.

2. Characterised by increased empathy and emotional expressiveness and decreased aggression. Also causes increased energy and euphoria. In higher doses may cause perceptual distortion and hallucination

3. Characterised by sensation of warmth, feeling of well being and euphoria with mild disinhibition at lower doses. Dysphoria, gross impairment of motor coordination and judgement at higher doses.

51)   THEME: EFFECTS OF DRUGS

Answers

1.   E. LSD

2.   F. MDMA

3.   I. Alcohol

Reference

Gelder, M.G., Lopez-Ibor, Jr. J.J., Andreason, N.C., (2000) *New Oxford textbook of psychiatry,* Oxford university press. pp 537, & 542.

52)   THEME: CULTURE BOUND SYNDROMES

Option

- A. Windigo
- B. Pibloktoq
- C. Khat
- D. Zar
- E. Koro
- F. Latah
- G. Amok
- H. Susto
- I. Dhat
- J. Brain fag

Select ONE option from the above list of options of culture bound syndromes that best describes each of the following clinical scenarios.

1. A condition prevalent among Malay men who presents with a period of brooding followed by an outburst of violence ending in exhaustion and amnesia.

2. A condition prevalent among Southeast Asian man presents with extreme anxiety and fear of involution of penis with fear of death.

3. A psychotic disorder common among Algonkian Indians presents with fear of becoming a cannibal through possession by a mythic creature.

52)   THEME: CULTURE BOUND SYNDROMES

Answers

1.   G. Amok

2.   E. Koro

3.   A. Windigo

Reference

Gelder, M.G., Lopez-Ibor, Jr. J.J., Andreason, N.C., (2000) *New Oxford textbook of psychiatry*, Oxford university press, pp 1062-1063.

53)   THEME: THEORIES IN PSYCHOLOGY

Options

- A. Bowlby's theory
- B. Cannon-bard theory
- C. Erikson's theory
- D. Festinger's theory
- E. Helmholtz theory
- F. James-Lange theory
- G. Kohlberg's theory
- H. Kelly's theory
- I. Lorenz theory
- J. Piaget's theory
- K. Schachter's theory

Select ONE option from the above list of theories that best describes each of the following statement.

1. Theory of personality that claims that all men are scientists in the sense that we put our own interpretation or theories on the world of events and we produce personal constructs.

2. Theory of development that claims that the mobile young animal in precocial species needs to learn rapidly to recognise its caregivers and to stay close to them.

3. Theory of moral and cognitive development that sees the child as an organism adapting to its environment, as well as a 'scientist' constructing its own understanding of the world.

53)   THEME: THEORIES IN PSYCHOLOGY

Answers

1.   H. Kelly's theory

2.   I. Lorenz theories

3.   J. Piaget's theory

Reference

Gross, R. (2001) *Psychology, the science of mind and behaviour.* 4th edition, Hodder & Stoughton. pp 619-621, 462-463 & 491-498.

54)   THEME: LEARNING DISABILITY

Options

    A. Prader Willi Syndrome
    B. Williams Syndrome
    C. Angelman's Syndrome
    D. Downs Syndrome
    E. Fragile X Syndrome
    F. Von Recklinghausen's Disease
    G. Rett's Syndrome
    H. Edward's Syndrome
    I. Cri-Du-Chat Syndrome
    J. Klinefelter's Syndrome
    K. Turner's Syndrome
    L. Lesch-Nyhan Syndrome

Select ONE of the above clinical syndromes which most clearly describes the following clinical phenotype

1. A 5-year-old boy presents with microcephaly, hyperreflexia and spasticity. He has hyperuricemia with clinical signs of gouty arthritis.

2. Short and obese young female with scoliosis and hypogonadism. Fasting blood glucose is 12.8 mmol/l.

3. A young boy presents with renal problems. On examination he has rocker bottom feet and micrognathia.

54)   THEME: LEARNING DISABILITY

Answers

1.   L. Lesch-Nyhan Syndrome

2.   A. Prader Willi Syndrome

3.   H. Edward's Syndrome

Reference

Gelder, M.G., Lopez-Ibor, Jr. J.J., Andreason, N.C., (2000) *New Oxford textbook of psychiatry*, Oxford university press, pp. 1954-1957.

55)   THEME: DIAGNOSIS OF COGNITIVE IMPAIRMENT

Options

    L. Delirium tremens
    M. Alzheimer's disease
    N. Vascular dementia
    O. Pick's disease
    P. Hypothyroidism
    Q. Lewy body dementia
    R. Pseudo dementia
    S. Creutzfeldt-jakob disease
    T. Normal pressure hydrocephalus
    U. Parkinson's disease

Select ONE option from the above list that best describes the clinical features of each of the following clinical scenarios.

1. A 58 year old woman was referred to you for "change in personality" and memory loss of 9 months duration. On examination she appears apathic, unconcerned and flat in affect but she denies feeling low. She has marked expressive dysphasia and sometimes repeats what you say to her.

2. A 69-year-old previously presents with increasing forgetfulness over the past two years. His wife tells you that he needs more help in dressing and bathing. She also has to look after all the finance, as he could no longer manage them.

3. A 43-year-old woman was referred with rapidly progressive memory loss and low mood. She is very disoriented in the interview and you notice frequent involuntary jerky movements of her right arm.

55)   THEME: DIAGNOSIS OF COGNITIVE IMPAIRMENT

Answers

1.   D. Pick's disease

2.   B. Alzheimer's disease

3.   H. Creutzfeldt-jakob disease

Reference

Gelder, M.G., Lopez-Ibor, Jr. J.J., Andreason, N.C., (2000) *New Oxford textbook of psychiatry*, Oxford university press, pp. 388-390, 406 & 417.

56)   THEME: DIAGNOSIS OF EATING PROBLEMS

Options

   A. Anorexia nervosa
   B. Bulimia nervosa
   C. Depressive episode
   D. Manic episode
   E. Psychosis
   F. Obsessive compulsive disorder
   G. Narcolepsy
   H. Prader willi syndrome
   I. Klein Levin syndrome
   J. Kluver-Bucy syndrome

Select ONE option from the above list of conditions that best describes the eating problem in each of the following situations.

1. A 23-year-old woman presents with symptoms of reduced appetite and weight loss. She says she lost interest not only in food but also "with everything in life". She weighs 9 and a half stone weight, has regular menstrual cycle and has no significant medical problems.

2. A young obese man presents with episodes of increased appetite and somnolence lasting for 2 to 3 weeks often associated with hyper sexuality several times in the past few years.

3. A 21-year-old 'bright' college student gradually became withdrawn, fell out of his friends and hardly left his room over the past 10 months. He also lost interest in his studies and failed to complete his university degree. He denies feeling low or having strange experience or hallucinations. He is "not bothered" to eat and lost more than a stone of weight over the past few months

56)   THEME: DIAGNOSIS OF EATING PROBLEMS

Answers

1.   C. Depressive episode

2.   I. Klein Levin syndromes

3.   E. Psychosis

Reference

Gelder, M.G., Lopez-Ibor, Jr. J.J., Andreason, N.C., (2000) *New Oxford textbook of psychiatry,* Oxford university press, pp 684, 1012 & 581-582.

57)   THEME: INVESTIGATION IN PSYCHOSIS

Options

    A. CSF Oligoclonal bands
    B. CSF for viral DNA
    C. Creatinine phosphokinase
    D. Clotting screen
    E. Urine drug screen
    F. Urine culture and sensitivity
    G. MRI Scan
    H. HIV tests

Select TWO investigations from the above list for each of the following clinical situation those are more useful in finding the aetiology. Each option may be used once, more than once or not at all.

1. A 32-year-old woman with no previous psychiatric history presents with sudden onset of euphoric mood, hyperactivity and reduced sleep. On examination she has extensor plantar response & sensory deficit in left leg. The left fundus appears pale & small.

2. A 27-year-old young man with no fixed abode was picked up by the police and admitted to a psychiatric ward after he assaulted a member of public in a shopping complex. He accuses that "people are out to get me" and was actively hallucinating. Physical examination was normal but blood sample was difficult to obtain, as his veins are thick and thrombosed.

3. A 24-year-old previously healthy man presents to A&E with 2 days history of headache, weakness or left arm and fever. He soon became very agitated, paranoid and possibly experiencing visual hallucinations. On examination, he appears confused, rigid and has extensor plantar reflexes.

57)   THEME: INVESTIGATION IN PSYCHOSIS

Answers

1.   A. CSF Oligoclonal bands
        G. MRI Scan
        (Multiple Sclerosis)

2.   E. Urine drug screen
        H. HIV tests
        (Drug induced psychosis/dual diagnosis)

3.   B. CSF for viral DNA
        G MRI Scan
        (Herpes Simplex Encephalitis)

Reference

Lishman, W.A. (1998). *Organic psychiatry, 3rd edn.* Blackwell science, Oxford, pp. 356 & 689-698.

58)   THEME: MANAGEMENT OF SIDE EFFECTS

Options

    A. Immediately stop the medication
    B. Reduce the dose and continue the medication
    C. Cautiously continue the same dose of medication
    D. Consider starting a different antidepressant
    E. Immediate admission to psychiatric ward
    F. Immediate admission to medical ward
    G. Weekly WBC blood monitoring
    H. Twice weekly WBC blood monitoring
    I. Daily WBC blood monitoring
    J. Urgent blood test for Creatinine phosphokinase
    K. ECG
    L. Immediate intravenous antihypertensives
    M. No action needed

Select the TWO most appropriate steps from the above list of options you would consider for each of the following clinical situation. Each option may be used once, more than once or not at all.

    1. A 42-year-old woman known to be suffering from Schizoaffective illness for several years is on Clozapine for two years now. She presents to her GP with malaise and easy fatigueability. Her WBC count is 3200/cubic mm.

    2. A 61-year-old known hypertensive is suffering from recurrent depressive disorder for more than 20 years and has been taking Amitriptyline for several years. He had a Myocardial infarction few weeks ago and had to be admitted to intensive cardiac unit for a week. He gets occasional chest pain, palpitation and dizzy spells and consequently is quite restricted in his activities.

3. A 21-year-old man was admitted to a psychiatric ward with first onset psychosis. He became very agitated and needed increasing doses of PRN Haloperidol. Few days later he appears very stiff, febrile, unsteady on his feet. His BP is 190/134 mm Hg but it was 70/42 mm Hg an hour ago when check by the nursing staff.

58)   THEME: MANAGEMENT OF SIDE EFFECTS

Answers

1.   C. Cautiously continue the same dose of medication
       H. Twice weekly WBC blood monitoring

2.   D. Consider starting a different antidepressant.
       K. ECG

3.   A. Immediately stop the medication
       J. Urgent blood test for creatinine phosphokinase

Reference

Schatzberg, A. F. & Nemeroff, C. B. (1998) *Textbook of psychopharmacology, 2nd edition*. American psychiatric press. pp. 707-709, 761-762 & 767.

59)   THEME: BASIC PSYCHOPHARMACOLOGY

Options

- A. Clonidine
- B. Diazepam
- C. Risperidone
- D. Atropine
- E. Glycine
- F. Glutamate
- G. LSD
- H. Nicotine
- I. Ketamine
- J. Paroxetine
- K. Acamprosate
- L. Ondansetron

Select TWO options from the above list, which has significant agonistic or antagonistic activity in the following receptors.

1. GABA receptors.

2. Cholinergic receptors.

3. NMDA receptors.

59)   THEME: BASIC PSYCHOPHARMACOLOGY

Answers

1.   B. Diazepam
        K. Acamprosate

2.   D. Atropine
        H. Nicotine

3.   E. Glycine
        I. Ketamine

Reference

Kendell, R.E. and Zealley, A.K. (1993) *Companion to psychiatric studies*, 5th edn. Churchill Livingstone, Edinburgh, pp. 121-136.

60)   THEME: THEORIES OF LEARNING

Options

A. Cognitive learning
B. Social learning
C. Positive reinforcement
D. Covert sensitisation
E. Shaping
F. Modelling
G. Incubation
H. Implosion
I. Aversion
J. Chaining

Select ONE option from the above list that is involved in the behaviour modification of each of the following individuals.

1. A chronic alcoholic man was given Disulfiram and asked to drink a pint of beer, under medical supervision. He became very sick and unwell. He decided to continue to take Disulfiram and remained abstinent over the next couple of years.

2. A young boy was observed to be fighting more frequent and more aggressive after playing a particularly violent video game. In the game, the player gets more points if he kills more people.

3. An 8-year-old boy suffering from enuresis started to use 'star chart' in which for every dry night he gets a silver star. Five Silver Star is equivalent to one gold star that will buy him a play station game.

**60)	THEME:	THEORIES OF LEARNING**

Answers

1.	I. Aversion

2.	F. Modelling

3.	C. Positive reinforcement

Reference

Gross. R., (2001) *Psychology, the science of mind and behaviour. 3rd edn,* Hodder & Stoughton. pp. 829, 690 & 162-164.

61)   THEME: ALCOHOL RELATED PROBLEMS

Options

   A. Acute alcoholic intoxication
   B. Alcoholic hallucinosis
   C. Wernicke's encephalopathy
   D. Korsakov's syndrome
   E. Alcohol withdrawal syndrome
   F. Alcoholic dementia
   G. Peripheral neuropathy
   H. Subdural haematoma
   I. Schizophrenia

Select ONE option from the above list for each of the following questions that best describes the clinical features.

1. A 65-year-old pleasant man was admitted to the surgical ward for hernia operation. Two days after admission, he became very irritable, restless and mildly tremulous. He also became sick twice but the physical and laboratory investigations were within normal limits except a mild increase in GGT.

2. A 45-year-old man was brought to A&E following an overdose. He tells you that he is "fed up of the voice" telling him over the past few weeks that he is a "liar" & "waste of space". He has been drinking heavily for the past 15 years and has a history of two inpatient alcohol detoxification programme.

3. A 62-year-old man was admitted for alcohol withdrawal treatment using reducing doses of chlordiazepoxide regime. During the second week of admission, you notice that his memory recall is very poor but other cognitive functions are relatively well preserved.

61)   THEME: ALCOHOL RELATED PROBLEMS

Answers

1.   E. Alcohol withdrawal syndrome

2.   B. Alcoholic hallucinosis

3.   D. Korsakov's syndrome

Reference

Gelder, M.G., Lopez-Ibor, Jr. J.J., Andreason, N.C., (2000) *New Oxford textbook of psychiatry,* Oxford university press, pp 490.

Lishman, W.A. (1998*). Organic psychiatry, 3rd edn.* Blackwell science, Oxford, pp 575 –584, 594-607.

62)   THEME: DEFENCE MECHANISMS

Options

    A. Passive aggression
    B. Schizoid fantasy
    C. Projection
    D. Denial
    E. Distortion
    F. Rationalisation
    G. Reaction formation
    H. Repression
    I.   Inhibition
    J.   Dissociation

Select ONE option from the above list of defence mechanism that has been used in each of the following clinical scenarios.

1. You are asking advice from one of your senior colleague for your forthcoming MRCPscyh examination. He tells you they test only your communication skills and "nothing else". He went on and said that it's a waste of money and he wouldn't sit for the exam. You later realised that he has attempted several times and has not yet passed the exam.

2. A 45-year-old woman suffering from a depressive disorder, currently under remission, when seen in out patient clinic tells you that her CPN doesn't like her and requests a change in CPN. You think that it's the patient who dislikes her CPN.

3. A 23-year-old young woman told her psychotherapist that she didn't remember anything about her childhood. After few months of psychotherapy, she now remembers that her uncle sexually abused her.

62)   THEME: DEFENCE MECHANISMS

Answers

1.   F. Rationalisation

2.   C. Projection

3.   H. Repression

Reference

Gelder, M., Gath, D., Mayou, R., and Cowen, P., (1996) *Oxford textbook of psychiatry, 3rd edition*. Oxford university press, pp. 135-136.

63)   THEME: THOUGHT DISORDERS

Options

    A. Flight of ideas
    B. Neologism
    C. Fusion
    D. Over-inclusive thinking
    E. Circumstantial thinking
    F. Crowding of thought
    G. Loosening of association
    H. Pressure of speech
    I. Perseveration
    J. Logoclonia

Select ONE option from the above list that best describes the following clinical example of thought process and speech.

1. When a young psychotic man was asked what drugs he was using he replies, "Heroin, health foods and cannabis"

2. A middle-aged lady was admitted to psychiatric ward for sudden onset of agitated behaviour. During the initial assessment when you asked her how long she has been unwell, she said "two weeks". When you asked her where she lives, she again said "two weeks".

3. You asked a young psychotic female where she works now. She replied, "I was trained as a nurse about 15 years ago, but I didn't like it and quit the job and was about to get a secretarial job but I got married during that time to a publican and decided to help him in business which didn't go well and so I decided to try teaching and I am working as a science teacher in a secondary school."

63)   THEME: THOUGHT DISORDERS

___

Answers

1.   D. Over-inclusive thinking

2.   I. Perseveration

3.   E. Circumstantial thinking

Reference

Sims, A. (2003) *Symptoms in the mind, 3rd edn.* Oxford university press, pp. 154-160.

64)   THEME: STAGES OF DEVELOPMENT

Options

  A. Oral stage of psychosexual development
  B. Anal stage of psychosexual development
  C. Latency stage of psychosexual development
  D. Phallic stage of psychosexual development
  E. Initiative Vs Guilt
  F. Basic trust Vs Mistrust
  G. Identity Vs Role confusion
  H. Intimacy Vs Isolation
  I. Preoperational stage of cognitive development
  J. Concrete operational stage of cognitive development
  K. Formal operational stage of cognitive development
  L. Sensorimotor stage of cognitive development

Select THREE options from the above list that corresponds with the developmental stage of each of the following child.

  1. A 4-year-old girl.

  2. A 14-year-old boy.

  3. A 9 months old boy.

64)   THEME: STAGES OF DEVELOPMENT

Answers

1.   D. Phallic stage of psychosexual development
        E. Initiative Vs Guilt
        I. Preoperational stage of cognitive development

3.   C. Latency stage of psychosexual development
        G. Identity Vs Role confusion
        K. Formal operational stage of cognitive development

3.   A. Oral stage of psychosexual development
        F. Basic trust Vs Mistrust
        L. Sensorimotor stage of cognitive development

Reference

Gross, R. (1996) *Psychology, the science of mind and behaviour.* 3rd edition, Hodder & Stoughton. pp 511-516 & 629.

65)   THEME: GENETIC ABERRATION

Options

   A. Down's syndrome
   B. William's syndrome
   C. Edwards syndrome
   D. Turner's syndrome
   E. Angelman's syndrome
   F. Rett's syndrome
   G. Cri du chat syndrome
   H. Fragile X syndrome
   I. Klinefelter's syndrome
   J. Huntington's disease
   K. Friedrich's ataxia

Select THREE options from the above list for each of the following genetic aberration with etiological significance.

   1. Trisomy.

   2. Deletion.

   3. Tri nucleotide repeats.

65)   THEME: GENETIC ABERRATION

Answers

1.   A. Down's syndrome
        C. Edwards syndrome
        I. Klinefelter's syndrome

2.   B. William's syndrome
        E. Angelman's syndrome
        G. Cri du chat syndrome

3.   H. Fragile X syndrome
        J. Huntington's disease
        K. Friedrich's ataxia

Reference

Gelder, M.G., Lopez-Ibor, Jr. J.J., Andreason, N.C., (2000) *New Oxford textbook of psychiatry*, Oxford university press, pp. 248-252.

66)   THEME: DIAGNOSIS OF EPILEPSY

Options

   A. Simple partial seizures
   B. Complex partial seizures
   C. Primary generalised seizures
   D. Secondary generalised seizures
   E. Myoclonic seizures
   F. Pseudo seizures
   G. Reflex epilepsy
   H. Gelastic epilepsy
   I. Jacksonian epilepsy
   J. Autonomic epilepsy

Select ONE option from the above list for each of the question below that best explains the clinical presentation.

1. A 64-year-old man known to be suffering from prostate cancer noticed some twitching movement of his left thumb. It gradually ascends involving forearm and arm before he loses consciousness. When he woke up, he felt weak in his left arm.

2. A 50-year-old woman suddenly complains of "strange feeling in tummy" and appears confused. Over the next 5 minutes, she is constantly pulling her clothes for no apparent reason and appears dazed. She has no recollection of what she did.

3. While listening to his favourite old song, a middle-aged man suddenly lost consciousness and developed tonic and clonic movements affecting his whole body. He later tells you that this has happened few times before while he was listening to the same song.

66)   THEME: DIAGNOSIS OF EPILEPSY

Answers

1.   I. Jacksonian epilepsy

2.   B. Complex partial seizures

3.   G. Reflex epilepsy

Reference

Lishman, W.A. (1998). *Organic psychiatry, 3rd edn.* Blackwell science, Oxford, pp. 237- 242

67)   THEME: DIAGNOSIS OF ANXIETY DISORDERS

Options

    A. Acute stress reaction
    B. Post traumatic stress disorder
    C. Agoraphobia with panic disorder
    D. Generalised anxiety disorder
    E. Phobic disorder
    F. Social phobia
    G. Depressive episode with anxiety symptoms
    H. Obsessive compulsive disorder

Select ONE option from the above list of anxiety disorders for each of the following clinical scenario.

1. A middle-aged woman started to avoid going to shopping malls and crowded places, as she feels "trapped". When she tried she became extremely anxious, shaky and thought that she was going to pass out.

2. A 35 year old man is frightened to leave his house and prefers to stay in. when he has to go out, he usually can't sleep the night before. When he leaves his house, he constantly worries about being observed by others, becomes tremulous & anxious and returns back without finishing the task. Recently he started to abuse alcohol.

3. A 49-year-old man developed feelings of sadness, inability to relax with poor appetite and loss of weight. He is very reluctant to go out and meet his friends because he worries that he may become tearful in front of them.

67)   THEME: DIAGNOSIS OF ANXIETY DISORDERS

Answers

1.   C. Agoraphobia with panic disorder

2.   F. Social phobia

3.   G. Depressive episode with anxiety symptoms

Reference

Gelder, M., Gath, D., Mayou, R., and Cowen, P., (1996) *Oxford textbook of psychiatry, 3rd edition*. Oxford university press, pp. 171, 173& 197.

68)   THEME: TREATMENT OF EATING PROBLEMS

Options

A. Typical antipsychotics
B. Atypical antipsychotics
C. Tricyclic antidepressants
D. SSRI
E. Mirtazipine
F. Benzodiazepines
G. Clomipramine
H. Family therapy

Select ONE most appropriate treatment option from the above for each of the following clinical situations.

1. A 34-year-old man is presented with 3 months history of low mood, anhedonia and loss of interest in his hobbies. He lost half a stone weight in and sleeps only 5 hours a day with early insomnia. He admitted having fleeting suicidal thoughts and has history of two overdoses in the past.

2. A 17-year-old girl is referred by her GP for weight loss. Her BMI is well below the average for her age and she looks very thin but she insists that she is very obese and in fact couldn't understand why she was referred to a psychiatrist. Her mom looks very anxious while her dad is unconcerned.

3. 30-year-old man recently lost his job, as he was 'frightened' to go out of his house. He said he drinks only fresh juice and 'nothing else' as he is constantly worried that other foodstuff may be contaminated with bugs. He admitted washing his hands several times, sometimes at night as well with consequent disturbance in his sleep.

68)   THEME: TREATMENT OF EATING PROBLEMS

Answers

1.   E. Mirtazipine

2.   H. Family therapy

3.   G. Clomipramine

Reference

Gelder, M.G., Lopez-Ibor, Jr. J.J., Andreason, N.C. (2000) *New Oxford textbook of psychiatry,* Oxford university press, pp. 726,848 & 827.

69)   THEME: SIDE EFFECTS

Options

A. Dependence
B. Hypotension
C. Polyuria and polydipsia
D. Bronchoconstriction
E. Agranulocytosis
F. Exacerbation of psoriasis
G. Fine tremor
H. Gross tremor
I. Hypomania
J. Hyperthyroidism
K. Hypothyroidism
L. Cardiac arrhythmias

Select THREE side effects from the above list of options that are more likely to be associated with each of the following drug. Each option may be used once, more than once or not at all.

1. Propranolol.

2. Lithium.

3. Amitriptyline.

69)   THEME: SIDE EFFECTS

Answers

1.   B. Hypotension
         D. Bronchoconstriction
         F. Exacerbation of psoriasis

2.   C. Polyuria and polydipsia
         G. Fine tremor
         K. Hypothyroidism

3.   B. Hypotension
         I. Hypomania
         L. Cardiac arrhythmias

Reference

British National Formulary.

70) THEME: TREATMENT OF SLEEP DIFFICULTIES

Options

A. Sleep hygiene alone
B. Short course of benzodiazepines
C. Maintenance benzodiazepines
D. Mirtazipine
E. SSRI
F. Amitriptyline
G. Methylphenidate
H. Dextroamphetamine
I. No treatment needed

Select ONE option from the above list that is appropriate in the management of each of the following situations.

1. A 19-year-old young man presents with daytime somnolence. On further questioning he tells you that he sleeps several times in the day usually for short periods of time, which is often irresistible. On few occasions, he suddenly "gave in" and fell down but didn't lose consciousness.

2. A 55-year-old man presents with excessive worries, difficulty in falling asleep and low mood of 2 months duration. He was referred to anxiety management training but didn't find it very useful.

3. A 65-year-old man has been feeling low, tearful and not sleeping well for the past few days since the sudden death of his wife. He is asking some help for his sleep.

70)   THEME: TREATMENT OF SLEEP DIFFICULTIES

Answers

1.   G. Methylphenidate

2.   D. Mirtazipine

3.   B. Short course of benzodiazepines

Reference

Gelder, M.G., Lopez-Ibor, Jr. J.J., Andreason, N.C., (2000) *New Oxford textbook of psychiatry,* Oxford university press, pp 1011-1012, 726 & 1290-1291.

71)   THEME: ALCOHOL RELATED DISORDERS

Options

    A. Adequate sedation
    B. Oral thiamine
    C. Oral multivitamins
    D. Intravenous thiamine
    E. Intravenous B complex Multivitamins
    F. Atypical antipsychotics
    G. Anti emetics
    H. Overnight observation alone
    I. Immediate admission to the medical ward
    J. No specific medical treatment

Select TWO options from the above list that are more appropriate in the management of each of the following clinical situation. Each option may be used once, more than once or not at all.

1. A 45-year-old man was taken to his GP by his wife after she noticed that he has become confused and unsteady on his feet over the past two days. On examination, he has nystagmus and conjugate gaze paralysis.

2. A 45-year-old man was admitted with low mood and ideas of self harm to the psychiatric ward. Three days after admission, he gradually became tremulous, anxious and was feeling sick. On that night he became increasingly anxious and tells the nurse that he could see "little people" in his room.

3. A 23-year-old man presents to A&E on Saturday night after he was involved in a fight. Breath analysis of alcohol shows very high levels and he appears unsteady. His physical examination is normal otherwise.

71)   THEME: ALCOHOL RELATED DISORDERS

Answers

1.   I. Immediate admission to the medical ward
        E. Intravenous B complex Multivitamins

2.   A. Adequate sedation
        G. Anti emetics

3.   I. Overnight observation alone
        J. No specific medical treatment

Reference

Gelder, M.G., Lopez-Ibor, Jr. J.J., Andreason, N.C., (2000) *New Oxford textbook of psychiatry,* Oxford university press, pp 386 & 496.

Lishman, W.A. (1998*). Organic psychiatry, 3rd edn.* Blackwell science, Oxford, p 597.

**72)   THEME: CONCEPTS OF PSYCHODYNAMIC
                       THEORIES**

Options

    A. Oedipus complex
    B. Transference
    C. Countertransference
    D. Projection
    E. Id
    F. Eros
    G. Thanatos
    H. Anima
    I. Animus
    J. Persona
    K. Imprinting
    L. Sexualisation
    M. Archetype

Select ONE option from the above list that best describes each of the following psychodynamic concepts.

1. Attitudes, ideas and feelings from the therapist's past towards significant people become transferred to acquaintances in the present, to the patient, often without justification.

2. A group of instincts regarded as basically destructive in that they seek to reduce us to inorganic matter.

3. The unconscious masculine side of the woman's female persona coming together with the feminine side in the concept of individuation.

72)   THEME: CONCEPTS OF PSYCHODYNAMIC THEORIES

Answers

1.   B. Transference

2.   G. Thanatos

3.   I. Animus

Reference

Bongar, B. & Beutler, L. E. (1995) *Comprehensive textbook of psychotherapy*, Oxford university press. pp. 27 & 30-31.

73)   THEME: PERCEPTUAL ABNORMALITIES

Options

   A. Functional hallucination
   B. Extracampine hallucination
   C. Reflex hallucination
   D. Completion illusion
   E. Autoscopy
   F. Hypnogogic hallucination
   G. Hypnopompic hallucination
   H. Paredolia
   I. Synasthesia

Select ONE option from the above list that explains the following abnormal experience.

   1. A 67 year old man suffering from Alzheimer's illness says that he experiences pain whenever he hears the words "coffee" and "clock" for the past few months.

   2. A teen-age boy says he can see a ghost's picture in his carpet in the floor that has plenty of cigarette burns. He describes it in an intricate and detailed fashion.

   3. A 48 yr old psychiatric In-patient says he can hear his fathers voice who is talking from half a mile from the ward.

73)   THEME: PERCEPTUAL ABNORMALITIES

Answers

1.   C. Reflex hallucination

2.   H. Paredolia

3.   B. Extracampine hallucination

Reference

Sims, A. (2003) *Symptoms in the mind, 3rd edn*. Oxford university press, pp. 96-113.

74)   THEME: UNCOMMON PSYCHIATRIC SYNDROMES

Options

- A. Capgras syndrome
- B. Couvades syndrome
- C. Cotard syndrome
- D. Fregoli syndrome
- E. Klein Levin syndrome
- F. Kluver-Bucy syndrome
- G. De clerambault syndrome
- H. Othello syndrome
- I. Ganser's syndrome

Select ONE option from the above list of syndromes that best describes each of the following clinical scenarios.

1. A 33-year-old man was brought to his GP by his mum with symptoms of acute abdominal pain and abdominal distension. Physical examination was within normal limits. His wife is 9 months pregnant and is currently admitted to Obstetrics ward for monitoring after she developed mild spotting.

2. A 28-year-old woman strongly believes that "the foreign secretary" is in love with her because he appears in TV news so that she could see him. She also claims that he is the father of her daughter and he is supporting her financially through disability allowance.

3. A 63-year-old woman stopped taking his anti hypertensive medications as she feels "pointless" because "my heart is rotten". Her husband tells you that she is "dull" and not like her usual self. She also stopped seeing her friends and has become more withdrawn at home.

74)   THEME: UNCOMMON PSYCHIATRIC SYNDROMES

Answers

1.   B. Couvades syndrome

2.   G. De clerambault syndrome

3.   C. Cotard syndrome

Reference

Sims, A. (2003) *Symptoms in the mind, 3rd edn.* Oxford university press, pp. 288, 133-134, 137-138

75)   THEME: MODE OF INHERITANCE

Options

    A. Huntington's chorea
    B. Rett's syndrome
    C. Down's syndrome
    D. Galactosaemia
    E. Acute intermittent porphyria
    F. phenylketonuria
    G. Lesch-Nyhan syndrome
    H. Prader Willi syndrome
    I. Creutzfeldt-Jacob disease

Select TWO options from the above list of diseases that are transmitted by each of the following mode of inheritance.

1. Autosomal Dominant disorders.

2. Autosomal Recessive disorders.

3. X linked disorders.

75)   THEME: MODE OF INHERITANCE

Answers

1.   A. Huntington's chorea
        E. Acute intermittent porphyria

2.   D. Galactosaemia
        F. phenylketonuria

3.   B. Rett's syndrome
        G Lesch-Nyhan syndrome

Reference

Gelder, M.G., Lopez-Ibor, Jr. J.J., Andreason, N.C., (2000) *New Oxford textbook of psychiatry,* Oxford university press, p. 1948.

76)   THEME: DIAGNOSIS OF MOVEMENT DISORDERS

Options

    A. Acute dystonia
    B. Akathisia
    C. Tardive dystonia
    D. Tardive dyskinesia
    E. Tardive akathisia
    F. Wilson's disease
    G. Petit mal seizure
    H. Epileptic fugue
    I. Complex partial seizure

Select ONE option from the above list of movement disorders, which describes each of the following clinical situations.

1. A 55-year-old lady known to be suffering from schizophrenia is on fortnightly Clopixol injection for several years. On routine outpatient clinic she repeatedly protrudes her tongue and pouts her lips for no apparent reason.

2. A 40 year old man known to be suffering from Schizoaffective disorder was recently started on Depixol 100 mg injection fortnightly. He is now complaining of "inner restlessness" and appears restless.

3. A 21-year-old man presents to his GP with gradual worsening of tremor and stiffness. During the consultation he appears disinhibited and makes dystonic movements, which is more marked in the upper limb. Blood investigations show grossly elevated liver enzymes but he denies any abdominal symptoms. He denies use of illegal drugs or alcohol and he is not on any medication.

76)   THEME: DIAGNOSIS OF MOVEMENT DISORDERS

Answers

1.   E. Tardive akathisia

2.   B. Akathisia

3.   F. Wilson's disease

Reference

Lishman, W.A. (1998). *Organic psychiatry, 3rd edn.* Blackwell science, Oxford, pp. 641-643, 253-254, -661-666

77)   THEME: DIAGNOSIS OF MENTAL ILLNESS

Options

A. Schizophrenia
B. Depressive episode
C. dysthymia
D. Bipolar illness
E. Generalised anxiety disorder
F. Phobic disorder
G. Adjustment disorder
H. Acute stress reaction
I. Post Traumatic Stress Disorder
J. Emotionally unstable disorder – impulsive type

Select ONE option from the above list of conditions that best diagnose each of the following clinical situations.

1. A 34-year-old man presents with feeling sad for three months with loss of appetite. He doesn't want to do anything and stays most of the time at home with very little motivation.

2. A 23-year-old girl complains of low mood for three years, chronic emptiness with history of multiple self-harm in the past. She was sexually abused in the past.

3. A19 year old college student presented with persecutory ideas, sadness, lack of concentration and perplexity. His academic performance has declined considerably over the recent few months. There was no evidence of hallucinations or thought interference. He also complained of lack of interest and loss of appetite.

77)   THEME: DIAGNOSIS OF MENTAL ILLNESS

Answers

1.   B. Depressive episode

2.   J. Emotionally unstable disorder – impulsive type

3.   A. Schizophrenia

Reference

Gelder,M., Gath,D., Mayou, R., and Cowen, P.(1996) *Oxford textbook of psychiatry, 3rd edition.* Oxford university press, pp. 197-99, 113-114 & 259.

78)   THEME: PSYCHOTROPIC MEDICATIONS

Options

    A. Amisulpride
    B. Amoxapine
    C. Chlorpromazine
    D. Clomipramine
    E. Clozapine
    F. Fluphenazine
    G. Olanzapine
    H. Quetiapine
    I. Maprotiline
    J. Trifluperazine
    K. Thioridazine

Select TWO medications from the above list for each of the chemical class of psychotropic medications.

1. Dibenzazepine antipsychotics.

2. Piperazine class of phenothiazine antipsychotics.

3. Tricyclic antidepressants.

78)   THEME: PSYCHOTROPIC MEDICATIONS

Answers

1.   E. Clozapine
        H. Quetiapine

2.   F. Fluphenazine
        J. Trifluperazine

3.   B. Amoxapine
        D. Clomipramine

Reference

Schatzberg, A. F. & Nemeroff, C. B. (1998) *Textbook of psychopharmacology, 2nd edition*. American psychiatric press. pp 200-201 & 310-311.

79)   THEME: MECHANISM OF SIDE EFFECTS

Options

    A. H1 Histamine receptors
    B. Alpha 1 Adrenergic receptors
    C. Alpha 2 Adrenergic receptors
    D. Muscaranic receptors
    E. Nicotinic receptors
    F. 5 HT 1receptors
    G. 5 HT 2 Receptors
    H. Dopamine receptors
    I. GABA Receptors
    J. TSH receptors
    K. Enzyme induction

Select ONE option from the above list that mediates each of the following side effects described below.

1. A 28-year-old young woman is known to be suffering from epilepsy was started on Phenytoin and she is now pregnant despite taking oral contraceptive pills.

2. A 45-year-old man suffering from resistant depression was started on Phenelzine after he failed to respond to two classes of antidepressants. Three weeks later he inadvertently ate some broad beans and became very dizzy, sweaty and collapsed. His BP is 190/130 mm Hg.

3. A 23-year-old man was admitted to a psychiatric ward with first onset psychosis. He was very agitated and needed increasing doses of PRN Haloperidol apart from his regular Olanzapine. 5 days later he appears very stiff, febrile, unsteady on his feet with fluctuating BP.

79)   THEME: MECHANISM OF SIDE EFFECTS

Answers

1.   K. Enzyme induction

2.   B. Alpha 1 Adrenergic receptors

3.   H. Dopamine receptors

Reference

Schatzberg, A. F. & Nemeroff, C. B. (1998) *Textbook of psychopharmacology, 2nd edition*. American psychiatric press. pp 439, 243-244 & 1020.

80)   THEME: DIAGNOSIS OF MEMORY IMPAIRMENT

Options

    A. Transient global amnesia
    B. Alzheimer's disease
    C. Subdural haematoma
    D. Anterograde amnesia
    E. Retrograde amnesia
    F. Factitious disorder
    G. Vascular dementia
    H. Dissociative amnesia
    I. Dissociative fugue

Select ONE option from the above list for each of the following clinical situation with predominant memory loss.

1. A 31-year-old man was brought to A&E by ambulance after he was involved in a car accident. During examination he couldn't remember the events happened in the previous 24 hours but he is oriented to time, place and person with preserved identity.

2. A 63-year-old known hypertensive man presents to an A&E department with headache and acute memory loss. He could tell you his name & address but his memory for remote events are better than the recent ones. When seen in the medical ward on the following day, his memory is intact.

3. A 21-year-old woman rang the police in a hysterical state alleging her boyfriend had assaulted her. She was taken to A&E where she said she couldn't remember her name and the personal details. Examination was within normal limits except a mild laceration of scalp. She appeared intact with coherent function and she was unconcerned about her memory loss.

159

80)   THEME: DIAGNOSIS OF MEMORY IMPAIRMENT

Answers

1.   D. Anterograde amnesia

2.   A. Transient global amnesia

3.   H. Dissociative amnesia

Reference

Kaplan, H.I and Sadock, B.J. (1995) *Comprehensive Textbook Of Psychiatry, volume I.* Williams & Wilkins, pp 638-642.

SUBJECT WISE INDEX

The Property of
Library Services
Hafan Derwen
Carmarthen

ISBN 1412026865
9 781412 026864